HERE IS WHERE WE DISEMBARK

HERE

IS WHERE

WE DISEMBARK

CLEA ROBERTS

Freehand Books gratefully acknowledges the support
of the Canada Council for the Arts for its publishing
program. ¶ Freehand Books, an imprint of Broadview
Press Inc., acknowledges the financial support for its
publishing program provided by the Government of
Canada through the Canada Book Fund.

Canada Council   Conseil des Arts
for the Arts   du Canada

Freehand Books
412 – 815 1st Street SW   Calgary, Alberta T2P 1N3
www.freehand-books.com

Book orders: Broadview Press Inc.
280 Perry Street, Unit 5   Peterborough, Ontario K9J 2J4
TELEPHONE: 705-743-8990 FAX: 705-743-8353
customerservice@broadviewpress.com
www.broadviewpress.com

Library and Archives Canada Cataloguing In Publication

Roberts, Clea, 1974–
Here is where we disembark / written by Clea Roberts.

Poems.
ISBN 978-1-55111-851-2

              I. Title.

PS8635.O2252H47 2010   C811'.6   C2010-903889-4

Edited by Robyn Read
Book design by Natalie Olsen, kisscutdesign.com
Author photo by Archbould Photography, archbould.com

Printed on FSC recycled paper and bound in Canada

PART I

PART II

A Note on the Text

Acknowledgements

A Note on the Author

Every step towards an origin is also
an advance towards a silence.

EAVAN BOLAND

Longing, we say, because desire is full
of endless distances.

ROBERT HASS

PART I

Transmutations

I

While we slept
the snow fell quietly
filling in the yard's
grey and brown truths
with explanation
of eider and light.

The white weight
you feel first
under the eyelids
before waking.

It carries you down
the path to the river—
the dark, rogue tongue
catching drifts
as you squat on the bank
small and bellowing
but muted.

Test to see how far
the voice carries
under the circumstance
and just how far
it peals into the forest—
knots of black branches
wearing the snow
like sleeves.

Then test to see how far
the words carry
and at what point
they come back to you
like small, hungry animals
capable of being tamed,
of haunting your windows.

II

We set out the ice lanterns,
feel the air's cold reluctance
in our throats,
skate slow, imperfect circles
on the lake ice
to its electric whimper,
the saw blade falsetto.

We are skating, we are dancing
because the mail strike is over,
because perfect white envelopes
arrive at our wreathed doors,
because peaches radiate
like gentled suns in the root cellar,
because this afternoon is dark
again, taking our dim
lamps to its breast.

Somersault into snowbank!
The empty thud of mittens
meeting in applause.

III

And there are days
that begin
with the sound
of trucks whistling
down the highway,
their J-brakes
a thick stutter,
the lonely
syllables of dawn.

Trucks bringing
the bread and the milk,
the table and chairs,
the newspaper,
the blue curtains,
whole lives in fact
or at least the pieces.

IV

The wind pulls snow
across the road,
armfuls of transient
white veil.

In the rear view
a raven shrugs
and flies off.

The sky is blind.
The road will carry you
a certain distance.

What is left
to understand?
You know
there is more ahead
than what is seen.

For instance,
the wrestle
with the wheel,
the convincing logic
of snow drifts
wrapping the tires,
pulling you softly
into a ditch.

V

Our house shudders
in the storm,
the snowflake vertigo.

There's a candle
on the table,
a talisman
or a lure.

We watch movies
with clever actors,
talk with friends
long distance,

put a log on the fire
and poke it
for good measure,

close the blinds
and dream
of the moon's
lean light.

VI

Moon when coyote
is my shadow.
Moon of the snapping
willow thickets.
Moon of the
missing cats.

Moon of the potluck.
Moon of tock, tock
at the woodpile.
Moon of filched
sleep.

Moon that raises our chins
with light years,
traces the camber
of a wing.

VII

And just as you remember
the winter you gave in,
you remember how you got there
walking to the mailbox
through a hoarfrost
the bright arteries of poplars
holding all the world's
light and space in their branches.

You were suddenly content
with your diminishing,
frayed boundaries
—the weather, its intent
and randomness
too big for you.

The boots were rated to -50 C
—you wore an extra pair of socks.

VIII

It was a thin winter
for rabbits, and therefore
a thin winter for lynx.

February ate
a cord of wood,
a snow shovel,
and a beaver hat.

The swans came back
when they came back,
their broad wings scraping
the sky with a sound
like breath panting.

And that afternoon
on Main Street,
while trucks idled
into a fog,
you bought
beeswax candles
and held the good story
of wood smoke
in your mouth.

The Necessary Element of Hunger

All day
the cows shuffle
in the cold wind.

The ground beneath
the cottonwoods
is dirty and roughed
with their hoof prints,
their pink nostrils
pushing steam over
their pungent coats
of shaggy rust.

How we hang
like spent marionettes
over the fence
watching them
their black marble eyes
blinking in the storm.

How it's not us, it's our hunger
that erects the fence post,
swings the gate closed,
nods its head at the scarecrow bricolage,
and walks back into the house.

When We Begin to Grow Old

I

Tell me the one
about the town
where you were born,
where the ocean
froze in the bay,
how it moaned and clacked
and collapsed with the tides
leaving its bright
and violent architecture
not much good
for skates.

II

It was a Friday.
On the way home from school
my sisters left snow angels
on every corner, like bread crumbs,
impractical totems, or
new, flightless birds.

At the back door
they flaunted the snow
under their collars
the hoary whiteness
stuck to their red felt coats,
the ligature of their bodies
pronounced
block to block and
all the way home.

Home

There's time to turn
back. A raven
pinwheels above
the canyon, one eye
holding me, trackless.

Nothing can hold the dusk
as it slips, the forgotten word
between mountains.

My lips, colder now,
purse against the pale blue air.

Walking the sawtooth
treeline I know
home is irrelevant.

This last light the residue
of a million years' journey
has been creeping
toward me, always.

Ravens

All day they fly
between the sharp hands of wind
dropping wood and water syllables—
enough to make us think
the frozen lake retreats,
the scrubby willows
have learned a new song,
the snow speaks oddly
to our feet.

Longest Night

Drunk with belief
and loneliness
we leave the
darkest bower
mumbling our
individual winters,
the cold so different
to each of us.

And each of us
having longed
in the deepest way
of the heart,
through hope
and the indication
of calendars,

might resent the moon's
second-hand light
that forgets to warm
our faces but fills
the snow tracks
of tree squirrels
with blue shadow
level as teaspoons.

Winter Equinox

Winter has carved
small caves
in our hearts,

pulled his boots off,
called up
for more snow.

A realization
that hurts a little,
makes our minds
anxious and full
of complaints,

like huskies
chained to their
dog houses,
their long whimpers
carrying further
in the cold.

A House is Built

I

When the sky
was our only ceiling,
when the trusses cut
hundreds of gem
blue windows
sharp with light,

when the smell
of pine and spruce
held it all together,
as we raced toward winter,
the snow that stays,
the ground freezing with resolve
to be that way forever
or for a season.

But before the ground freezes,
plant some trees.

The beaver,
she'll take three dozen.
She's building
a house too.

II

It's cold and we come to the site
with armloads of firewood,
more tools, and our muscles
like recovering amnesiacs
always remembering more
of themselves.

The basement warms first,
we bring down lawn chairs
and dub it Mexico,
consider the air miles
on the credit card,
consider the depth
of fatigue and ache,
as our work boots
become supple
with the heat
from the stove.

III

Even with masks
we're high on the fumes.

And every night
of slinging and staining boards
we've argued, muzzled
against each other
and the chemical air.

It's so good
to be ignorant
of your grievances.

By the time
I stow the brushes
in paint thinner
and you start the truck

there's nothing ahead
but a yellow line
on the road, and deer,
their white tails
falling and rising
in the peripheries
of the headlights.

IV

I dream of wooing
drywallers.

Strong, honest men
who answer their cell phones.

Their ball caps, eyelashes,
even their words
coated with a fine
layer of dust.

They occupy
the air above us.
They swagger on stilts—
hang drywall,
spread mud,
sand everything
to white.

How humbly
we hear our footfalls
in the porcelain light
of new rooms so full
of damp and acoustic air,
fans scanning and humming
in agreement.

V

The dog herds
cement trucks
down the driveway.
She's never had it
this good.

V I

Valentine's Day you give me
bats of pink fibreglass insulation,
an itchy feeling at my wrists and neck.

But before that
we sweep out a corner,
share good bread, a fondue
over the camp stove.

Outside the chimney smoke
is combed white
against the night.

We are merry
and undiluted.

VII

This house is a place
touched everywhere,
even the bones.

This house is built
according to the body
and what it dreams.

House of the uncut grass in June.
House of the bathtub and the nailbrush.
House of the indelible.
House of the first born.
House of the long necks of larkspur,
metronomes in the wind.

Cathedral

And that is what we almost believed in
that winter, we almost believed
in heaven and all its permutations
as you fiddled dog biscuit, house key—
the artifacts of the known world
in your pocket
and I walked beside you,
breathless, arms swinging,
the baby in the pulk
shushing behind me,
the sad and the angry and the peaceful
rooms inside the decisions we'd made,
and the poplars so remarkable
in their thin, white gowns,
while the prints of all the creatures
crossed paths at their feet.

Winter Ticks

They say the moose
are shingled with ticks,
ticks that gorge
at the neck and flanks,
ticks that make
the skin itch.

It's the catastrophe
of distraction:
can't eat, can't sleep—
eighty thousand
winter passengers
each taking
a thimble of blood.

Trade a winter coat
for a forest
of rough-barked trees,
it lets the chill in,
the dewlap shudders,
the haunch stone cold.

Bed down
upwind from hunger
and still hunger finds you:
a flurry of paw prints, wing tips,
entrails radiate, the violent flower
of skin and bone.

Weight

This is where I find her
dropped on the trail
like a mitten dipped
and heavy with ice.

The dog spins around us
its pink tongue
the envelope of its intellect
every fibre of its coat stiff and white
and the barrel of its chest
heaving grey air.

I feel like the weight of snow
as it slides from a roof
and slumps to the ground
but really it is the moment
of the fall I inhabit
which is taut, endless,
until I shake her shoulder,
see the eyelash flutter.

Saving someone
is a terror I feel on the cellular level
my body's chemical tremble
so full of the residue of intent,
the recognition I made a hair appointment
then took an early lunch
before my walk in the woods.
That's all it took
to become a deciding factor.

She is not the hero,
I am not the hero—
this is all I know
as we sit in her kitchen drinking tea
and I touch her thighs and arms
thick with cold.

Rendezvous

I don't need
a hairy-leg contest
to tell me it's been a long winter.

But there's a contest
for everything
this time of year—
turkey bowling,
wife carrying,
dog howling.

Last night—
a talent show
at the Capital
where Sam bisected
an airborne melon
with a chainsaw.

Which topped
the mummified cat
on display, the one
found during renos,
desiccated in its last moments
of fury.

After the show
we stayed on for drinks,
talked about shovelling
the day's dump of snow
tomorrow.

Already the white banks
were building in our minds,
the growl of the blade
scraping the driveway.
There was so much of it
we wondered
if we'd ever catch
our breath again.

Pine Grosbeaks

In February
even borrowed
colour is welcome.

Birds as red
and plump as apples
bob in the pine trees,
sharpen their beaks,
dream fine, green buds
months away.

Spring Equinox

Loose threads
of migrating birds.

Shadows of bears
in the field.

The forest rattles
its bones.

The Brown Season

Light returns
and we want winter gone.
But it's slow to go
and hangs on the land
like a bad friend,
like a bruise, first dark
then brown and yellowing.

The snow recedes off the road,
clings to the north side of ditches.

How much it has concealed from us,
how heavy-handed and unfair it was,
how it coveted the canoe,
the spare snow shovel,
the old cat curled tight as stone,
the grass, ill-coloured,
licked and wet like the subject
of some great beast's affection.

A Song Like Heels Clicking

Before the first thaw redpolls
take the wind like a trick,
fly their awkward half pipes,
hang in the trees like revellers
too early for the party.

We fill the feeder,
we measure light in minutes.
The husk of winter blows away
and afternoons extend themselves
in paper-thin increments

to the pasque flower
raising its weary, purple head,
to staccato of studded snow tires on pavement,
and to mud, never so exotic,
tracked across the kitchen floor.

First Thaw

Song of the unzipped parka,
song of the dangling fur mitt
swinging in time.

Song of the shopkeeper
chipping the snow pack
from the sidewalk.

Song of snow melt
gurgling in the downspout.

Song of the boot
testing the ice.
Song of the wet boot
walking home.

Song of gravel
plinking at the windshield.
Song of fishtailing
and chucking slush
and near misses.
Song of the snowmobile
saying was, was, was.

Song of all the birds
I'd forgotten.
Song of dogs and children
amok between
the matronly hands
of hockey nets.

Song of the man
stranded on the roof
with a snow shovel saying
Hello? and Ladder?
and Anybody? and Jump?

Song of a long winter
breaking itself open,
slicking our driveways,
cueing the perennials too soon.

Walking on the Path by the River

Spring is sudden here,
but slow, a slow, old dog
that catches your eye,
walks behind a couple
wearing sweaters
tied luxuriously
at their waists.

Winter's chandeliers
fall on the stony riverbanks
and the ice floes whisper
*go buy lemons
and meet me at Laberge—
the lake's heart
is open.*

The Small, the White Feathered

Driving on the
Skagway road toward
spring, spark the snow buntings,
wing chips of light
in tight circle swing.

Spring is here,
take down your half-melted
ice lanterns and
re-tire the truck.

The roadside ditches lined
with the small, the white feathered
pecking the road salt,
the infant shoots.

Paradigm of Flood

The soft ground loves me
kisses the heels of my galoshes
with mud and leaves.

The corner store
saturated with people.
They buy kindling, rub shoulders,
contemplate the treble hook pixie lure.

Clouds crouch between mountains,
cling and weep to trees, low flying planes.

Cottonwoods stiffly line the riverbank—
grey and burdened with crow.

We muster
the lead-heavy mud dance,
walk out for the mail,
come back full of rain.

Seasonal Adjustments

I

So many things grow
unasked.

Garlic in the kitchen.
Crocus in the compost.

And love, it waits in the cupboard
with the potatoes
its eyes exploding with flowers.

11

The cottonwoods
shake out their buds
obscuring the mountains,
the granite petals
that surround us.

III

At dusk
bats flutter, echolocate,
snap hawk moths
from the sky.

We force our campfires and tents
make the new, fumbling
gestures of love,
while the wind loses its teeth,
picks a tune across
the old valley floor.

IV

Easter Sunday,
the kids strung out
on candy.

They wander the streets
rain-slicked kicking
stones and frogs.

Today they are five or six
and generous with the world.
They love babies
too much, walk dogs
fiercely on tight leashes—
small wind-ups,
boots scuffing
up and down
the road.

V

This garden makes
a more difficult journey
than others.

Small, nut-coloured birds
covet the grass seed

while the dog digs up
the potatoes,
feels her paws
pulling through the soil,
recognizes this
as love.

The green beans
only an inch high
nod quietly
under the weight of slugs.

Black Bear at Pelly Crossing

She's rousted from sleep
gluey-eyed but quick,
heartbeat accelerating
like a motor.

The wind brings
news of a man
and she enters the world
as destroyer,
a shadow with its own
dark velocity.

If a bear dreams,
she's dreamed the gunshots
and she's dreamed
her cubs screaming and falling
from trees
like pieces of night.

And she's dreamed
the charge
to the juncture
of tooth and bone
where she won't bluff,
the slug blooming in her heart,
the kinnikinnick
rustling beneath her.

Summer Solstice

Upstairs the bed made, the quilt turned back.
But who thinks of slumping into new dreams
when it's the season without darkness,
and every evening the sky at dusk
can only consider night.

Somewhere a dirt bike whines
through the forest opposite the river.
Somewhere it chokes and is not heard again.

And the chit, chit, chit
of the sprinkler
like the drunk at the party
beginning the conversation
over and over.

And the stand of poplar
fenced against the beaver—
its leaves shimmer and click
as if in applause.

At solstice we clomp onto the deck
drink retsina and watch the sky
like a dog doing improbable tricks.

The backwards flip, the tap dance,
the spontaneous operatic, all more believable
than the myth of night.

Commute in Summer

Suddenly, the ice
is gone from the rivers
and the summer workers
are riding their bicycles.

The gravel crackles
under their tires
as they swoop
through the streets
clean and bright
as gulls.

They are commuting
to their summer jobs
in shops and hotels
where things are uncomplicated.
They punch tills or make beds
and take their lunch hour
in the park
by the clay cliffs.

Somewhere 10,000 hectares
of forest are burning
but the smoke
hasn't reached us,
just the CBC news.

Canoes float by
on roof racks.
I'd rather be on the river,
but the shape
of a keel is a consolation of sorts
and the prettiest thing

I've seen—that,
or the pink haze
of fireweed growing
out of a burned forest,
or how a cyclist
must raise her hip a little
and renew her grip
on the handlebars
before she pedals away.

Country Residential

Hang left at yesterday's
pink party balloons
limp with cold
and tied to a post.

Pass the mailboxes
with posters advertising
lost cats and snow removal.

Pass three horses
pumping their thick, agreeable heads
like oil derricks
and a skinny, yellow husky
barking at the rustling pines
or barking at the other dogs barking
or just barking for no reason at all.

This is my neighbourhood—
where fences run like erratic statements
supported by unreliable facts,
where we've beaten out
a space for ourselves,
where people decorate their yards
with woodpiles and automobiles,

where despite us, the harrier hawk pauses
to hover and pluck mice from the field,
and the red fox waits out the day in a culvert,
and the white-tailed deer peruses
our vegetable gardens at night,
and the blue bird perches and flicks
on the telephone wire like a piece of ribbon
cut from the sky.

Whiskey Jack, Grey Jay

I take the path along the water
because it's summer
and the lake is not frozen
but filled with lily pads
that bob and tug as the wind
pricks the black surface.

Dusk is a grey bird
with a song that is everywhere.
It spooks the last light
off the tree tops, cools the skin
with long, rogue feathers,
perches between the tree of day
and the tree of night.

Nature of Nature

Because it was so unctuous
and quick to skitter
I did not expect
the chipmunk to return
headless, body stuffed
like a pocket watch
in the soft mouth
of the old dog.

It was a fair hunt
and precise too,
the chipmunk snapped
quick as a twig—
the perfect red shoe
dropped at my foot.

Even in sleep
this is an earnest dog—
paws that twitch
at dream velocities
and the tight, deep howls
and silly whimpers,
the tuning and retuning
of the instrument
of longing.

River Camp at Little Salmon

When the canoe slows to shore
I take the rope, wait for the bow's
gravel breath.

All day the river
has carried me uncomplaining,
would take me further
if I stroked back to the current.

This morning it promised
the rapids at Stone Mountain
navigable, the Stewart Estuary
not in flood.

At camp it made me
strange to my nakedness
my skin numb, not my own
in the cold, silty water.

And in the evening
the river floated
small voices to my campfire
from the fish camps upriver,
brought the cow moose
to the water to drink.

Sunset, Little Atlin

I

The light
has chosen
a path across
the water.

The heart is tight—
pulls to the horizon
like an easy fish
on a line.

11

Look—
every shadow
has a colour.

Stay and rest
in the thin
shawl of dusk.

What to Carry With You

In August of the year that
ruined and saved us
we ride toward autumn
on the Fish Lake road,
the road that climbs to the treeline
where the shrubs are small-leafed
and hunkered down
because the eager wind is here, always,
keeping the berries slow.

Soon the lakes will ice
and the theatre will open
and we'll know friends on Main Street
only by the colour and trim of their parkas.

And in our homes
light will become finite and coveted,
as we resign ourselves
to the tender clink of teapots
retrieved from cupboards,
and the atonement of wood
popping and cracking
in the fire.

From the Northeast, as a Thought Would

Summer has turned—
you are more nostalgic than depressed,
longing for the slow, easy language of snow.

The last poplar leaf
conducts the wind—
a wind that occurs from the northeast,
as a thought would,
one that has waited its turn
and now bolts full of intent
like a winter hare or a crack
in the windshield.

A twitching nose,
the insinuation of frost
pushing up soil,
wedging things apart.

Cool hand of fall
resting on your shoulder.

Fool Hen, Ruffed Wood Grouse

Call yourself a fool to think
it was your own heart making
a drumbeat escape to the woods.

When your heart is perched 10 feet
up a black spruce
what do you say?

It cocks a black eye at you,
becomes a bird again
and you say: simple creature.

Laundry Day

A deer ruminates
in the field.
Chops thaw
on the counter.

I separate the lint givers
from the lint takers.

I work quietly
coiling garden hose
while the dryer vents
eloquently into autumn air.

Somewhere dog and fox circle,
consider the food chain,
disengage.

PART II

Arrival

1. In which Daniel Snure addresses his imaginary
wife in the autumn of 1897

Here is where we disembark,
at Hootalinqua in the moonlight.

Your eyes flash like trout fry
and your smile,
lovely as a sprung trap.

It's dark, the town is still,
but we are greeted
by the loose tongue of alder smoke
which tells me the Hän women
cure salmon for the winter—

you will learn this too,
though the dance hall music
still clings to you
like black fly in spring.

But this is Hootalinqua.
We have a police post,
a telegraph office, and a shipyard
where the paddlewheelers winter,
dream of the forests they will burn
in their bellies next year.

You are among us
and you are welcome.

2. In which Mrs. Snure responds

Men float by on rafts
made of wood from old cabins
and borrowed rope.

I watch from the porch—
they do not stop here
much at Hootalinqua, their sails
hundreds of rough-edged
postage stamps
pulling down river.

If only we got mail
regularly.
Here it is monthly,
we get grizzlies
more often.

I have begun
to feel lonesome
and virtuous
when I hear the bear dogs howl,
even the mean ones.

And you are tender
and more lonesome
and you watch me
as I check for my eyebrows, my lips
in the mirror above the sink
of the married quarters.

Load

1. In which Mrs. Martha Purdy comments on
appropriate attire for hiking the Chilkoot Pass

I recommend a cord skirt
cut above the ankles.

It's warm and fetching,
and practical for stepping over
dead horses on the trail.

There are dead horses
every 15 yards
from Skagway to Bennett—bloated
and eviscerated by the carrion eaters,
their hollow eye sockets
do not watch us as we go.

But they follow us
in their own way, the stench
sewn into us, a gut string of memory.

The living horses are spooked
all the way through the Pass,
packing our creaking grubstakes,
stumbling on the roots of trees,
their thick hides shuddering
to relieve themselves of flies.

At night, when the wind shifts
you can hear the sound
of small rock slides on the mountain,
a sound like hoofs
clipping and clopping
fitful and wild.

2. In which the Pass responds

You and your retinue
got through this time
before I let down
my load of rock and snow.

You don't see me hanging
and weighted above you.

You are staring at the heels
of the cheechako in front of you,
breathing so hard you can't hear
the sound of my mass shifting
as you crawl up my skirts
like a line of ants.

I'll take your body
a quarter mile before
I break it completely.

I will love you widely
plucking trees and
boulders as I go.

Breakup

1. In which a woman addresses the river

I was a half-believer
in the myth of water.

All winter I heard the river ice
whimper and stretch in its bed.

I could speculate on breakup
and the first boat to water
but not the weight of the ice
as it flips and squawks,
or how the water
wears it like a skin, reptilian
or how the sound of it
is like a large crowd
whispering and breaking dishes
as it goes.

It's three weeks before my steamer
heads for Dawson
stopping only at wood camps
where axes clip the air like coughs
and the forests are diminished
to log piles.

Where the channels are shallow
I feel the tug of a sandbar
like a nag, a hand on the shoulder
pulling me back.

2. In which the river responds

Last summer
I took the paddlewheeler Kaska,
my slow kiss, my fury,
exploding on its hull.

Like others
you dream of the gold
I drop in the shoals
of my tributaries.
With the same care
I let the caribou pass
their antlers rocking
silver under the moon.

Today I am owned.
They dig me out,
make my creeks and streams
crude and blatant.

And still, I deliver you
against the current
of my better judgment.
I will plant you
where my milky waters
pool and slow,
feel the music of your steps
cross to shore.

Claim

1. In which Miss Ada addresses a man of known immoral character

I'm fourteen,
plain and humourless
as an egg.

There's a ball of spruce pitch
in my skirt pocket for sucking.

I'm fourteen,
I know there is a name
for everything.

There is a name for every steamer that docks,
every foot of shore on Hunker Creek,
every rock and flower I pick,
what you put in me
up there on the berry patch
sometimes twice in an afternoon.

By the time the forests and boardwalks
moan and snap with cold
my belly is remarkable

and father's outrage is complete.
It settles and clings over town
like wood smoke.

2. In which the known immoral character responds

For no good reason
I feel entitlement
to your pious, awkward
body stepping across
the grey frost field
in a boiled wool cape,
slow and jerky
as a wood grouse.

I want to swing my whole weight
into you like an axe, I want to feel
a release like river ice
at breakup scraping the shore clean
of last year's willow
so everything heaves
toward the unclaimed
part of you.

Harvest

1. In which a king salmon addresses a woman fishing

The pebbles creaking
tell me everything.

That you are tired of waiting
for the nets to fill.

That you shift your weight
from the left foot to the right
before speaking.

And when you speak
it is with prayer
as if to catch me
with your gratitude.

And you tell me cousin frog
waits in your net
with a new story
of slower currents
and wider eddies.

You know it's all I think of—
the slow, shuddering journey
to the creek bed
that I know without knowing,
weaving upriver,
the moon just a shiver
between the trees.

2. In which the woman responds

A fish scale moon
clings to the trees.

My small boat
tied to the weir.

Your dorsal ridge
casts a muscular, furious light
against the water,
black and lapping
as my arms
pull in the net.

You are a gift
against hunger.

You hang from your gills
on the fine knots
my mother taught me.

Stone eye, belly of roe,
you are a piece of river current
cut loose with my knife.

Downstream
the village drifts
in alder smoke.

Listen, old girl,
they are
calling us home.

Lure

1. In which a N.W.M.P. sergeant comments on
the residents of Paradise Alley

Reeking of perfume
they compel the attention
of respectable women,
toss oranges and trinkets
to the children.

They are sturdy,
rough as lumber,
promising as a heap of pay dirt,
built for service
and not the virtuous kind,
hanging from the doorways
of their cabins
one arm swinging
or the hips swinging,
the silk curtains and red lanterns
floating a little in the breeze.

Last week one hired
the Ferguson boy to fetch matches
and he loved her so much
he punched her in the stomach
when she paid him
with a kiss.

And I see the girls
their heads turning
as they walk past the Alley
rolling their hoops astray and
finding stones to kick
as the whores brush out
their blonde and brunette wigs.

2. In which Sweet Marie responds

It's true
I depend on the
lonesome, flexing
desires of the men
from the creeks.

They think
we are both free
but I do not own
this cabin,
the crimson chemise,
or even my body
because I traded it
for the passage.

I hate the taste
of their fingers
sour as coins.

It's only 8 p.m. and already
I am carved out
like a cheap rattle
while outside
the boardwalks
still creak.

Who would deny me
the pleasure of giving
something I do own:

a spinning top made from tin,
a piece of saltwater taffy—
all for the small
and discreet smile
of a child, running off
with her head down,
peering into
cupped hands.

Caption

1. In which Pearly MacMillan addresses her photographer

Take the photograph
that makes me
permanent
in this world
the one I send home
with letters, a pinch of gold dust,
a few Indian trinkets.

They'll never know
that everything is borrowed:
the silk dress, the rifle,
the bags marked gold
and filled with gravel,
the empty whiskey crate
where I rest my
high button shoe.
There's even
a sled dog in harness—
temporarily loyal
and whining for scraps
by my side.

I smile convincingly, subtly
the gunpowder flash
occidental, intoxicating,
mine.

2. In which the photographer responds

This studio—
a repository of hope.

The glass negatives
rattle with intentions
as I pace the floor
looking for props.

Today you are my 3 p.m.,
my frontier gal,
the portrait
that pays the rent.

Every day I drop the cape
and lift the pinhole shutter.
I take the photograph.
I take the outline
of heroics.

But inside, we are dust
like the mountains around us—
treeless, featureless,
ground down,
too many shovels
turning the earth.

Bad

1. In which Babe Wallace, known prostitute,
addresses her daughter

I fell into dreams
as dawn growled
through the window.

You wore innocence
outside like a shield
threw firewood, an old bucket, stones
at the wolf who'd come for the chicken
the one that hadn't laid
since snowfall.

You feed rosehips to the thoughtless
beaks of birds,
and figure the grey mass
of fur and tooth
a simple equation,
watch it lope away
toward the Indian camp
at Moosehide.

All afternoon
you patrol Front Street,
stopping to jab a stick
in the snowbank
looking upriver
shouting
bad dog.

2. In which her daughter wonders

Men come to our house.
Even as dusk settles
its shadowy haunches
she opens the door.

She must be a priest of sorts,
a necessity.

Upstairs they make sounds
that devour the stars, still the wind.
A sweaty air grinds in the hallway
smells of lamp oil
and unwashed skin.

I pull my sheets
to my earlobes.

I hear a bored, grey voice say,
My, what big teeth you have.

Prayer

1. In which Nellie Cashman addresses the resident ghost

We aren't a godless people,
we're resourceful.

And maybe that's why
we believe in you too.

Our first altar
was made of crates
and flour sacking.
After service, parishioners
crossed themselves
all the way home
because somewhere
you were watching.

I can see you
in the washbasin reflection.
You rattle the windows,
you gather the dogs in packs
and set them loose on the children.
You rot eggs and sour milk
on the way home from the store,
you have an unnerving accuracy
for detecting a weak heart
and jumping on it.

You are the pale sister,
the one who walks the underside of river ice,
brings the horse and dog teams
crashing through for company
the fray eventually subsiding
leaving only the black current
which disappears and disappears
under the ice floe.

2. In which the ghost responds

I want to be the creases
in your bedclothes, the kinks
in your unbraided hair,
the morning smell of your breasts,
of sweat, of talc, a little smoke
and rose water.

I want to be the crumbs
from your toast, the ones
you brush from your mouth
before you turn the pages
of last month's newspaper.

And later, I want to be
the frost tightening
your eyelids, nostrils,
as you chop kindling
and sweep the stairs
to your boarding house.

As you leave
the crowded church
I want to be the steam
rising off your shoulders.
I want to be the ground
wherever you stamp your feet
into drifts, and the sunken sound
of your beaver mitts
beating off the cold.

I want to be his hands
jerky and earnest
as sled dogs in harness

when he comes to your room
on a Sunday,
those sounds between you,
something like a lake warbling
or a raven throwing out its vowels
one by one.

Laundry

1. In which Mrs G. I. Lowe addresses her woodcutter

The lye soap
splits and dries
the skin,
my fingertips open
like wood grain.

If I spoke your language
I would first ask you
how your shirt
was kept so clean,
because I want to know
about your women.

Then I would ask you
if there is a name
for the music
kindling makes
as you drop it
in my wood box.

You dispel the heavy smells
of prospectors, their deepest odours.

You bring me
the smell of balsam,
the wind between the jack pines
where the caribou chew moss,
the smell of the alder smoke
from your fish camp.

2. In which the woodcutter responds

Each day I must
walk farther for wood.
The paddlewheelers
are eating the forest.

And look at your red hands
on the washboard,
the perspiration
on your small, square brow.

Have you always worked
this hard for strange men?

Do they know about the gold dust
that settles in your washtub?

Their dirty shirts roil and gesture
in the pots on your stove—
pegged to your line,
they are sharp flags snapping
at my neck as I go.

Twitch

1. In which a woman addresses a wolf at the Stewart
and Yukon River confluence

How far did I wade
into the blue light of dusk
to see you canter cross-river,
rabbit and grouse
swinging like pendulums
from your wicked, disastrous jaw?

You measure seasons in hunger,
the thin bones buckling, the last
ligament twitch, the soft,
open muscles of the cavity
of longing.

Sometimes I think
your ear catches on my breath,
before you slip between the spruce and pine
quiet with winter's resolution:
the snow-burdened bough,
the resin ice-brittle.

My excursion, my distraction, my intruder.
My husband is sleeping, I have nothing
to shake off the winter's scurvy but you.

Fatigue accumulates like a snowdrift,
every day I test my teeth with my tongue
and watch you slip between the trees.

2. In which the wolf responds

Before I've left the forest,
stepped out onto
the frozen river,

I hear you stamp your feet
against the cold
and the weary elocution of ice.

You wear the beaver
on your hands,
nestled tight and pink
as new kits.

I want to take you with me—
your sweet face white as ash, narrow as a deer's.

There's a longing that tugs at my neck,
makes my ear twitch.

Birth

1. In which Grace Anderson addresses her husband
at Claim #63, Eldorado Creek

Wake up,
the buntings
are skimming the creek
and I think it will snow soon.

There's a thin layer of ice
in the sluice boxes
and the pickaxe handle
is furry with frost.

I've got a child
growing inside me.
Last night she thrashed
like a king salmon
in my belly
as the wood smoke
curled and curled
above the cabin roof top
and the aurora above it
a slow, green whip.

How long until the
small fists beat at my chest
for milk and I become
unravelled in the smell
of her, the small hours
of undecided light
at dawn, the pain
of my life all at once
narrowing and expanding?

2. In which her husband responds

She's smaller than
I thought, frog-like,
mewling then crying,
then wailing,
won't take the milk,
even at $8 a quart.

I'm told I will love her
but how much
can you love
a replacement?

There was nothing we could do
but watch the blood bloom
under the bed sheets,
outside the sound of shovels
pitching into dirt
and the windlasses creaking.

I remember the morning
before the birth, how you turned
so awkwardly in bed
with such a lovely burden
to talk about the coming snow,
something as inevitable
as the narrowing light.

How I bathed you
in the tub how these
same hands dried your body
as you pointed to the cradle
the pile of receiving blankets
the empty, white window.

Fire

1. In which a good citizen argues in favour
of relocating the whores to Lousetown

Fire is a moral issue
that indicates
the combustible
nature of sin.

We call them
women-of-the-town
and it is well known
that their lamps burn
the longest.

Yesterday
two thousand men
blasted fire breaks
with dynamite,
pulled buildings
apart with ropes.

When the fire advanced
they lugged chattels
into the cold night
until you could not see
the men, so black with soot,
only a table, a chair,
a player piano
disappearing like
dumb puppets
out of the fire's
terrible light.

This town is tinder.
She'll go up again.

2. In which the fire responds

All night
the wind shouldered
the buildings
on Front Street
so much they
shifted and creaked
in the gusts.
The parlour lampshades
swayed in agreement
that it was the perfect
night for a fire.

So I ignited the creosote
in the chimney
leapt out of the Green Tree Saloon,
had taken a bakery, a hotel
before the river ice was broken
and the first buckets of water
were filled and cast.

I called the miners
in from the creeks
with my smoke,
I made the malamutes
howl in their yards.

The frenetic townspeople
tried to stop me
but the flaming false fronts
bowed like generals
and the wall tents lit
quick as paper hats.

Liar

1. In which Kate Carmacks addresses her husband
at Bonanza Creek

I married you, took
my dead sister's place,
the girl who shared
my blanket.

I make you bone butter
and bannock, snare the tender
necks of rabbit and wood grouse
for our stews. I take in laundry
when nothing shows up
in the pans.

Gold fever—
it's a kind of devotion,
one that catches you
like the pain of a burn,
makes your heart jump
at the site of every creek mouth,
makes you dream of fish
with scales of gold coin.

What have you
brought down on us, husband?
These new people
with fancy shoes
step off the boats,
their pale faces
already searching.

Today the Tr'ondëk Hwëch'in
sent their songs away.
They aren't safe here
anymore.

2. In which George Carmacks, credited discoverer
of gold, gets the last word

Because the truth is
interchangeable
as socks,
I'm not regarded
as a good source.
My stories are made
from the whole cloth.

My woman tells me
to talk right. She's from
the wolf clan—
they've known the trickster
since he stole the sun.

I take all her ways
but this one,
I eat her meals,
I wear her skins,
I learn the air trembles
at the caribou crossing,
and that even dark skin
tightens in the cold.

I take all her ways
but the truth:
you never know
when you'll need
a different ending.

A Note on the Text

The poems in Part I are set in Yukon and Northern British Columbia.

The poems in Part II are set during the Klondike Gold Rush, 1897–1898.

■ ■ ■

Colophon

This book is set in FF Seria and the accompanying sanserif, which were designed by Martin Majoor in 2000.

Acknowledgements

My gratitude to the Yukon Foundation, the Yukon Government's Advanced Artist Award Program, and the Canada Council for the Arts for grants that enabled the creation of these poems.

Thanks to the editors of the magazines where versions of some of these poems first appeared: The Malahat Review, The Dalhousie Review, The Antigonish Review, Lake: A Journal of Arts and Environment, Ice-Floe: International Poetry of the Far North, The Northern Review, and Event.

A special thanks to Sharon Olds and Eamon Grennan for their generosity, time, and for reading and commenting on drafts of the poems in this collection. Thanks to everyone at the Atlantic Centre for the Arts. Thanks to Sharon Thesen for correspondence and friendship and for helping me see these poems a little better.

Thanks to Melanie Little for guiding this book to Freehand. Thanks to Robyn Read for her thoughtful work as editor and to Sarah Ivany and the editorial collective at Freehand for their support.

Thanks to my friends and family in Canada, Switzerland, and England: the Robertses, the Girouards, the Ainsworths (and Peter Bruhin), Mary MacDonald, Bonnie and Carson MacDonald, Eric

Hegsted, David Stouck, Susanne Behrens and Dave Waldron, the Eineigels, Liz Parker, Valerie Ireland, Marusia Heney, Astrid van der Pol, Joanna Lilley, Jamella Hagen, Rona Aasman, Peter Emerick, Barry McKinnon, and Donna Kane.

With love, "Transmutations" is for Jean and Linnea Roberts, "Cathedral" is for Bonnie MacDonald, "Sunset, Little Atlin" is for Ben, Donna, Yara, and Garrett Ainsworth, and "Prayer" is for Susanne Eineigel.

Thanks to the rivers and dogs that carried these poems.

And finally, my deepest thanks and appreciation are for my husband, Mark Roberts, who paddled while I casted, and who provides such generous encouragement and support for my writing. This book is dedicated to him.

A Note on the Author

Clea Roberts lives in Whitehorse, Yukon
on the Takhini River with her husband
and daughter. Her poems have appeared
in The Antigonish Review, CV2, The Dalhousie
Review, The International Feminist Journal
of Politics, Lake: A Journal of Arts and Envi-
ronment, The Malahat Review, Prism Inter-
national, and Room. Roberts has received
fellowships from the Vermont Studio
Centre and the Atlantic Centre for the Arts,
and is a three-time recipient of the Yukon
Government Advanced Artist Award. Her
work has been nominated for a National
Magazine Award, and her poem "When
We Begin to Grow Old" won the After Al
Purdy Poetry Contest. Roberts co-organizes
the Whitehorse Poetry Festival.